# Dunfermline and Rosyth in old picture postcards

by
Eric Simpson
and
George Robertson

European Library – Zaltbommel/Netherlands

*Cover picture:*
The cover photograph reveals, rather intriguingly, a ghost-like figure behind the tripod-camera. It shows, too, the south side of the abbey prior to the removal, in 1905, of part of the Wardlaw vault. This alteration meant that the fine south processional doorway became visible again, after having been concealed for three hundred years.

*The authors:*
George Robertson, a former Police Inspector with Fife Constabulary, was born in Rosyth and has remained in the Dunfermline area for all of his life. He is a voluntary guide for the Dunfermline Heritage Trust.
Eric Simpson, a former Head of History at Moray House College in Edinburgh, has lived in Dalgety Bay since 1966. His publications include 'The Auld Grey Toun – Dunfermline in the time of Andrew Carnegie 1835-1919' and 'Discovering Banff, Moray & Nairn'.

*Acknowledgements:*
Most of the postcards and photographs are from our own collections. We are grateful, however, to those people who loaned us material and/or assisted in other ways. While it would be impossible to list every person who helped in one way or another, special thanks must be paid to the following: Edith May, Andy Lawrence, John Hunter, William Brown, Freda Drysdale, Nadia and Angelo Maloco, Anne Rushton, Jean Wright, George Luke, Fraser Simpson, the Carnegie Dunfermline Trust and staff, Chris Neale and Dunfermline Library staff. We are also indebted to our wives, Kathleen and Maureen, for proof-reading and assistance. We must also thank the Royal Commission on the Ancient & Historical Monuments of Scotland for permission to reproduce the cover photograph.

GB   ISBN 90 288 5538 6 / CIP

© 1993 European Library  –  Zaltbommel/Netherlands  –  Eric Simpson and George Robertson/Dunfermline

No part of this book may be reproduced in any form, by print, photoprint, microfilm or any other means, without written permission from the publisher.

# INTRODUCTION

Today Dunfermline is a thrusting industrial and commercial centre. It is also, however, a burgh with a long and proud history. Its royal connections go back at least to the time of Malcolm Canmore (1057-1093). Around 1070 Malcolm married the Saxon princess Margaret, who established a Benedictine monastery at Dunfermline. This abbey was richly endowed, as its associations with Margaret, who was canonised in 1249, made it a place of popular pilgrimage. Since Margaret had been buried at Dunfermline, other members of the royal house also wished to be buried there. Dunfermline was the last resting-place, it has been estimated, of no fewer than eight monarchs, four queens, five princes and two princesses.

The most notable of these monarchs was Robert I. It was the clearing in 1818 of old foundations for a new parish kirk that led to the rediscovery of Bruce's tomb. Patriotic fervour led to the plans of the new kirk being altered to enable the words KING ROBERT THE BRUCE to be cut in stone on the parapet. The 19th century church was built end-on to the nave of the medieval monastery. This Norman-style nave had survived because it served as the parish kirk until the completion of the New Abbey Church in 1821.

Nearby are the substantial remains of the monastic guesthouse. In the Middle Ages, monarchs frequently stayed there. During those periods of residence, Dunfermline became, like other similar places, the seat of royal authority. In the 16th century the guesthouse was converted into a royal palace for the use of Anne of Denmark, the bride of King James VI. Their second son, the future Charles I, was born there, the last monarch to be born in Scotland. Another medieval survival is the Maygate building, which has long been known as the Abbot's House. This historic building is now being adapted to house a major new heritage centre.

The closure of the abbey, at the time of the Reformation, was an economic setback for the burgh. So too was Jamie the Saxt's departure for London, following his accession to the English throne in 1603. In 1624 came another major disaster, when most of the town was devastated by a sudden outbreak of fire. Nearly one hundred years later, Daniel Defoe described Dunfermline as a town in a sad state of decay. But, by then, the seeds of recovery had been sown, thanks to the development of the linen industry. By the mid-18th century, Dunfermline was noted for its textiles, manufacturing 'tablelinen of all kinds, ticking, carpets, and striped woollen stuffs for women'. When Thomas Pennant visited the town in 1772, he found a thriving and rapidly expanding town. There were, he estimated, around one thousand hand-looms at work in the town and neighbourhood.

When he bridged and culverted the Tower Burn in 1770, George Chalmers, laird of Pittencrieff, opened up part of his estate for a 'new town'-type development. This bridge and causeway were commemorated in McGonagall-style verse:

> *This Bridg did cost five thousand pound*
> *by Mr. Chalmers paid,*
> *And all to beautify the toun,*
> *from it he sought no aid.*

Increasing prosperity, thanks to the demand for coal and locally produced textiles, encouraged this kind of expansion. It was the fine linen industry above all that laid the basis for this era of growth. By the 1830s the Dunfermline manufacturers were employing some three thousand hand-loom weavers, working mainly in their own homes or in small workshops. The Dunfermline specialities were damask patterned tablecloths and napkins. In consequence, the population of the town and suburbs more than doubled between 1801 and 1841, reaching 13,323 by the latter date. Unfortunately, Dunfermline and its weavers went through a period of disastrous decline in the 1840s. Many hand-loom weavers were forced to seek employment in other trades or to seek new pastures. William Carnegie, hand-loom weaver and Chartist agitator, was one of the victims of the economic depression. Selling his looms, he and his family left to try their luck in the U.S.A. While Will Carnegie himself could not adapt to the New World, his bright, thrusting son, Andrew, certainly did. By the ruthless exploitation of his Pittsburgh-based steel empire, Andrew Carnegie became one of the richest men in the world. When in later years he started to disburse his fortune, Dunfermline, the town of his birth, was one place that benefited to an inordinate extent.

The hand-loom weaver's cottage, where he was born, now forms the basis for the updated and fascinating Andrew Carnegie Birthplace Museum. But most of the weavers' cottages and small workshops, and the hand-looms they contained, were swept aside when, in the second half of the 19th century, the linen industry was transformed. New markets and new manufacturing techniques revitalised the fine linen trade. The linen manufacturers switched from the hand-loom to the power-loom, thus ensuring a period of dramatic growth for both the industry and the town. The smokestacks of the new large factories and their deafeningly-noisy steam-powered looms symbolised the new age. Built in 1851, Erskine Beveridge's St. Leonard's Mill, with its two high lums, was the largest. By the 1880s Erskine Beveridge & Co had around 1,200 employees in its largely female workforce. Prior to the outbreak of the First World War in 1914, there were more than 6,000 workers in the eleven linen mills. The growth of the town and rising prosperity were reflected in the new public buildings that were erected – like the flamboyant, locally-financed townhouse of 1879 and the Carnegie-gifted public library and swimming baths. Carnegie's most spectacular benefaction came when he purchased Pittencrieff estate, and then in 1903 gifted it for a park. This was accompanied by a huge endowment fund, to be administered by trustees 'to bring into the monotonous lives of the toiling masses of Dunfermline more of sweetness and light'.

Because of the threat posed by an enlarged German fleet, the British Admiralty decided in 1903 to build a naval base, with adjacent dockyard, at Rosyth. To house incoming workers, new houses were built on ground close to the dockyard. In 1911 the burgh boundaries of Dunfermline were extended to include the new, planned 'garden city' of Rosyth. Although not complete when war broke out in 1914, the naval base and dockyard played an increasingly important role as the war progressed. In 1917 the main British battle force, the Grand Fleet, was transferred from Scapa Flow to Rosyth. In the Second World War and during the Cold War too, when the USSR was perceived to be a potential enemy, the Rosyth base was of great strategic importance. Since the end of the Cold War, the reduction in defence expenditure has meant that the future of the naval base and dockyard is open to question.

For much of the interwar period, the dockyard had been on a 'care-and-maintenance' basis only. These were very difficult times, as the coal pits in the immediate area were worked out and the staple industry of linen damask weaving had also collapsed. Fashion changes and competition from man-made fibres posed too many problems for the fine linen industry. Some of the textile mills were turned over to silk manufacture by Swiss firms seeking to avoid the onerous customs duties imposed when Free Trade was abandoned. Today, although some textile manufacturing survives, no linen, nor silk either for that matter, is woven in Dunfermline.

In the second half of the 20th century, new industries, including electronics, brought renewed growth and expansion. The town and the district as a whole benefited from the construction in 1964 of the Forth Road Bridge. In 1975 local government reorganisation brought the history of the burgh as such to an end, the ancient burgh being incorporated in Dunfermline District.

With 1993 being the 900th anniversary of the death of St. Margaret, Dunfermline will once again be a destination for pilgrims. This little book, it is hoped, will help both residents and latter-day pilgrims to see how the town looked in the not too distant past and to comprehend how and why it has changed.

1. The number of smartly dressed pedestrians and bystanders in this late 1920s High Street scene begs the question. Was this a special occasion? The number of people spilling on to the roadway points to a low traffic density. A solitary motor-car and a tram-car are the only vehicles to be seen. Although the tramway system has gone (closed down in 1937), the ornate Gothic-style townhouse, which was completed in 1879 at a cost of £20,000, still fills a useful purpose. The chain store on the extreme left belonged to the then American-owned F.W. Woolworth & Co. Ltd. It was opened in 1922.

2. This frontal view of 'Woolies' 3d. & 6d. store was obviously taken at Easter time, as the windows are stacked with chocolate Easter eggs. At that time it was 'Woolies' boast that 6d. (sixpence) was their maximum price. This building was 'Woolies' original Dunfermline store. The business was transferred to the north side of the High Street in 1938. The electric cables for the tramway system are clearly indicated. The causey sett surface of the road stands out very clearly. This picture reveals that the footpath, though, appears to have been formed of ribbed concrete.

3. This photograph of the High Street, with 'Woolies' again very much in focus, was taken on a sunny day as the south-facing shops have their sun shades down. Since, in contrast to the first illustration, the Glen gates are visible in the distance, the photograph was taken some time after 1929. The car in the foreground, which looks like a Morris Bullnose, could well be the same vehicle that appears in the first photograph. Woolworth's employees in those days started work at 9 a.m. and continued till 7 p.m., except for Saturdays, when they worked till 9 p.m. On Wednesdays, though, they had a half day off.

4. There are no cars to be seen in this turn-of-the-century view of the High Street. The store on the extreme right belonged to Nicol, the hatter. As is evident from this picture, and from most of the others at that time, hatters and milliners did good business then and for many years thereafter. The pavement is up and there are men working outside the building next door which is evidently still in process of construction. Built originally for the North of Scotland Bank in 1898, it is now the Clydesdale Bank.

5. The building which preceded the above can be seen in this even earlier photograph. John Jamieson & Co. sold 'ready made clothing' from the shop on the ground floor. This shop and its neighbour to the right were subsequently demolished. Their late-Victorian replacements were much more ornate.

6. On the other side of the street, the Dunfermline Press office, with its corbie-stepped gable, was one of the surviving older-style buildings. The Press advertised that they were photographers and engravers as well as printers. Around that time Sanders' City Restaurant, later the Bruce Restaurant, specialised in Scotch Shortbread and Carnegie Rock. Their premises included 'Ladies' Afternoon Tearooms and Lavatories' and 'Cycle Accommodation and Smoking Room'. This is now where Boots, the Chemists, have their premises. Two types of delivery vehicle are visible – one a small horse-drawn spring-cart; the other, with the big basket on top, seems to be a large hand-cart. The wicker basket looks like one of the containers that commercial travellers used for their samples. As with the two previous photographs, this picture was taken prior to 1909.

7. On the other hand, this photograph was taken in, or after, 1909, because that was the year when Dunfermline's tramway system came into operation. The initials D.C.I. on the tram stood for Dick's Cooperative Institutions, which was a retail firm with many branches in West Fife. Although privately owned, it paid a dividend, which at one time amounted to 4/- in the pound. The tartan and white heather surround is a common feature in Scottish cards of this period.

8. The same part of the street appears in this view, but it was photographed when the pillars carrying the overhead tramway cables had been erected, but before the lines had been laid down. It could be that the baskets outside the Royal Hotel contain the hotel's laundry.

9. An advertisement-card for the Royal Hotel with, we presume, the proprietor and family standing at the main door, and other members of the family, or perhaps staff, up on the roof. The carriage-and-pair at the door, with smart top-hatted driver, conveys the message that this is a classy establishment. In contrast to the previous view the window-curtains are, for the most part, tidily bunched. The ornamental glass on the cornerdoor and on the adjacent window reveals that this was the public bar. Not surprisingly, there is no wheel-barrow to be seen in this formally arranged photograph. The hotel was closed in 1962 and demolished two years later to make way for a supermarket.

10. Barrows were widely used for all sorts of purposes earlier this century. There are at least four to be seen in this circa 1900 postcard. An array of wide-brimmed hats is on display in what is probably a milliner's shop on the left side of the view. This is the High Street but looking in the opposite direction this time. Tyler's at No. 5 High Street, on the right, sold boots and shoes.

11. Tramcar No. 2, which was delivered in 1909, is seen here heading west along the East Port loop. The building on the corner of East Port and New Row was built in 1912 for the Bank of Scotland. The bystanders blethering at the top of the New Row are evidently in no danger from fast-moving traffic.

12. East Port again with a pair of tramcars this time. The direction board on the leading car, No. 12, shows that Townhill was the destination. A youth in Boy's Brigade uniform is to be seen on the left. As was common in those days, he wears a sturdy pair of boots. The sender of this postcard was a First World War serviceman, who had been picked for a draft bound for France. He, Jim, requested Bell (presumably his wife) to send on his towel, shirts and socks as he was required to show them before he left for France on the following Monday. Although it was posted in 1916, this postcard must have been old stock as the Bank of Scotland, which was completed in 1912, does not appear in this view.

13. An eastward view along East Port. There is a wide variety of postcards on sale at the shop on the left. The present-day Robins Cinema is located to the east of this shop, which was occupied by John M. Bryce.

*East Port Street, Dunfermline*

14. This tram-car is bound for Cowdenbeath. It is clearly not a busy time of the day as there are plenty of empty spaces on the top deck, which, as with all Dunfermline cars, was open to the skies. This particular car (No. 3) was delivered in October 1909. In the early 1920s the tram-car destination boards were switched to a position just above the driver's head.

15. We now go back along the town's main thoroughfare. Bridge Street comes into view to the west of the City Chambers. At the far end of Bridge Street, which was at that time one of the best shopping streets in Dunfermline, can be seen some Chalmers Street buildings, which were demolished in the late 1920s to make way for a new formal entrance to Pittencrieff Park.

16. In this turn of the century view we see A. & D. Hoeys' high-class drapery emporium which was located where Bruce Street adjoins the High Street. Although the sun-shades are up, the frame which supports the corner-window shades is just visible. Nearly every inch of glass is used to display the wide variety of articles on sale. The gentleman standing at the High Street door is probably one of the shopkeepers. There is, however, another gent standing looking out of the corner-window at first floor level. Is this the other Mr. Hoey?

17. Assorted boxes and packages and lots of children, some of them barefooted, are to be seen in this early Chalmers Street scene. A sign on the left side of the street draws attention to a 'Public Telephone Call Office'. In the wee sweetie shop on the right, Fry's Chocolate is on sale. Previously known as 'the Pit Paith', the name Chalmers Street was formally adopted in 1809.

18. The same street some years later, probably around 1914. The tram-cars have arrived. On the extreme left is Coull & Matthew's, ironmongers. This was their first shop, opened in 1911. The shops on the opposite side include Ferguson, the florist. This shop was opened in 1911. The Labour Exchange is located in the same new block. It was later transferred to the East Port. Labour Exchanges were established in Britain in 1909 by an Act of Parliament which was passed by the Liberal Government of the day. The church – then United Free – on the right side of the street (in the centre of the card) was demolished within recent memory to make way for a public car park.

19. Dewar Street, with Chalmers Street in the distance, was at the turn of the century a residential suburb. The children, eleven girls and one boy, are well dressed. With only two gas lamps on this part of the street, it would have been hardly well-lit.

20. Park Avenue, on the south side of the town, was an even more upmarket street. The errand boy would have been delivering messages to one of the big houses in the area. He stands apart from the other children, who once again are mostly of the female sex. The wee boy in the centre of the group is dressed in a then fashionable sailor's suit. The two ornate lampposts were almost certainly symbols of authority – in all likelihood marking the home of the then Provost of the burgh.

21. In contrast, the more traditional-style buildings in Abbot Street show the usual town centre mix of back street shops and tenements. The Abbot Street buildings we see here were demolished prior to 1912 to make way for local authority administrative offices.

22. This is the corner where Guildhall Street meets Abbot Street. The fruiterer and fishmonger advertises 'Fresh Fish Daily'. The watchmaker next door (P.R. McLaren at No. 25) was also an optician. He sold jewellery, too, specialising in 'Ladies' Hatpins and Scotch Jewellery'.

23. Abbot House, which appears in the distance in the previous illustration, comes closer into focus in this Edwardian-period postcard. As elsewhere in the Auld Grey Toun, the streets were surfaced with causeys. Historic Abbot House is now being adapted for use as a heritage centre.

24. Elgin Street looking towards Nethertown Broad Street. The Bothwell Linen Works (1865) are located on the right side of the street. The terminus of the Nethertown branch of the narrow-gauge Elgin Railway was located in the gap site on the west side of the street. This branch was opened in 1834 for goods and passenger services. By the time of this photograph, the passenger service had been discontinued and the area was used as a coal depot. The view of Dunfermline Abbey, as seen from the Elgin Railway, brought tears to the eyes of the young Andrew Carnegie when, en route to the U.S.A., he and his family departed from their beloved Dunfermline in 1848.

Birthplace of Andrew Carnegie, Esq., LL.D., Dunfermline....

25. The dwelling where Andrew Carnegie was born in 1835 was a popular photographic subject. When Carnegie, one of the world's richest men, turned philanthropist, he gave vast sums of money to his native town. The portrait here, however, was gifted by Henry Clay Frick. It was Frick who in 1892 brought in armed Pinkerton agents to smash a strike at Carnegie's Homestead Steelworks. In the ensuing conflict, ten lives were lost. Although Carnegie was holidaying in Scotland at the time, his reputation suffered. The shop on the left of the central cottage-style building was later demolished as was, too, the building on the extreme right. It should be noted that the cottage was divided into two. The house on the left was the part occupied by William and Margaret Carnegie. When this photograph was taken, the house on the other side was occupied by a butcher named Donaldson. The chimney of the 19th century gasworks can be seen protruding behind the cottage.

26. Moodie Street, with Carnegie's birthplace on the left, is shown here in a postcard with a postmark dated May 1908. The shop shown in the previous photograph had gone by then. Note the causey setts with the flat, smooth tracks to allow for easier movement of cart wheels. Around that time, the Dunfermline Journal Printing Works, advertising its products, stated that there was: 'A Nice Selection of Post Cards Always at Hand at Mr. Carnegie's Birthplace, Moodie Street.' The property had a few years earlier been purchased by Andrew Carnegie: it was subsequently transferred to the Carnegie Dunfermline Trust. The original visitor's book survives. The first visitor, from Edinburgh, signed the book in August 1908. In the following year, Carnegie himself paid a visit, writing in the book: *First visit to my birthplace / The humble home of honest poverty / Best heritage when one has a heroine for a mother.*

27. Moodie Street from the south with the Carnegie Memorial Hall (1928) on the right. It was Carnegie's widow, Louise, who had this hall built. Its original purpose was to house and display ornamental caskets, addresses, and other honours conferred on her husband.

## OPENING ANNOUNCEMENT.

# A. MALOCO

Begs to announce to the public that he has Opened the Shop situated at

## 27, SOUTH INGLIS STREET

AS A FIRST-CLASS

## Fish and Potato Saloon.

Fresh Fish Daily, Quality Guaranteed.

**Fish Suppers, 3d. each.**

**A FIRST-CLASS BILLIARD ROOM**

Up-to-Date Tables by Burroughes & Watts.

28. The Carnegie family emigrated to the U.S.A. in 1848 to better their lot. When, at a later date, a number of Italian immigrants came to Dunfermline, we see the reverse process at work. Angelo Maloco was one of the successes. In 1904, about four years after arriving in the town, Angelo, as we see from the advertisement, opened 'a fish and potato saloon' with 'first-class' billiard-room attached. Six years later, in what was then a time of local prosperity, he opened larger premises on the south side of the High Street.

29. In this picture, the proud proprietor Angelo Maloco stands on the extreme right of the group, with, on his right, his son Leo and daughter Guiseppa. On the far wall, what looks like a picture is actually an internal window, with just visible another daughter and a member of staff. The business continued in the family until 1985 when the premises were sold for redevelopment.

ENTRANCE GATES, PITTENCRIEFF GLEN, DUNFERMLINE. (20)    A.357.

30. Carnegie's most notable benefaction to the town of Dunfermline was Pittencrieff estate, which he purchased in 1902 and handed over to the care of trustees in the following year. The ornamental gates which provide the main entrance to Pittencrieff Park, or the Glen as it is popularly known, were completed in 1929. Erected in honour of Louise Carnegie, they bear the name of the donor's widow. The formal opening of the gates was conducted by three local schoolgirls, all called Margaret, which was the Christian name also of Carnegie's mother, daughter and grand-daughter. To facilitate the construction of the gates a number of properties in Chalmers Street and Bridge Street were demolished.

31. 'My new title beats all. I am Laird of Pittencrieff...' With these words, Andrew Carnegie celebrated the purchase of Pittencrieff estate. Believing by this time that the rich were merely trustees of the wealth that they had acquired, Carnegie gave the park to the townsfolk of Dunfermline, together with an endowment fund to be used 'to bring to the monotonous lives of the toiling masses of Dunfermline more of sweetness and light...' Pittencrieff House itself, which now incorporates an interesting museum, dates back to the early 17th century. This picture is early 20th century.

32./33. As these postcards indicate, Pittencrieff Glen quickly became a popular place of resort for the people of Dunfermline. The trustees appointed by Andrew Carnegie to administer the park and the endowment fund organised open-air concerts in the Glen. A temporary wooden band-stand was erected and a band formed.

316. The Band Kiosk, Pittencrieff Glen, Dunfermline.

The band kiosk shown in these two postcards was erected in 1909 and replaced the original temporary structure. This kiosk was replaced by the present Music Pavilion in 1935.

34./35. Postcards of the bandstand were popular with visitors, so much so that Valentine & Sons, Ltd. of Dundee, updated the card on the left by removing those people who were wearing outmoded garments. The most obvious alterations were the removal of the two women in the centre foreground and the addition to the group

THE BANDSTAND, PITTENCRIEFF GLEN, DUNFERMLINE.

in the foreground (see the right-hand card) of a young woman dressed in a white flapper-style costume. Since male fashions had not radically changed, no alterations were necessary in that respect. Doctoring cards was, it should be said, fairly common procedure.

36. Another popular facility was the Glen tea room. This postcard shows the Tudor-style tea room which the trustees had erected in 1904. With the number of customers exceeding the available space, the tea house was extended just three years later.

37. This postcard, which was posted in 1910, shows the extended tea room with the old stables and Pittencrieff House in the background. In this winter-day photograph there is not a single person to be seen.

38. Tea in the Glen continued to be popular, so further enlargement was evidently deemed to be necessary. This attractive bungalow-style building was replaced by the present tea house in 1927.

39. The tea room, which replaced the bungalow-style building, appears to the left of the Music Pavilion. The replacement tea house was opened in 1927 and the new pavilion in 1935. It is obvious from the number of spectators that band music was as popular as ever.

40. A peacock, long dresses, a uniformed gent (a 'parkie'?) and an invalid in a wheel-chair are some of the 'sights' in this old postcard, where we see too the old tea house in the background. The substantial stone-built building on the right once housed the stables. The stable-block was destroyed by fire in 1936. Subsequently, an ornamental garden was laid out on the site.

41. The Eagle's Cage was another attraction. Although there is no longer an eagle on display, there is still a small aviary at Pittencrieff Park.

42. Squirrels were then another captive species on view to the public. The Squirrels' Cage, as shown here, no longer exists. However, grey squirrels roam freely in the heavily wooded Glen, providing a source of entertainment for today's visitors to the park. With regard to the swings, the sexes are separated as this Edwardian period card clearly shows. Inscribed on the top spar of the right-hand set of swings is the stern admonition: 'Reserved for girls under fourteen years of age.'

43. Adults no doubt appreciated the splendid floral displays in the walled garden adjacent to Pittencrieff House – shown here rather unusually in a gable-end view. This photograph would have been taken soon after the purchase of the estate in 1902. The Carnegie Dunfermline Trust later had this area covered by glass houses, displaying exotic hothouse plants.

44. At one time the main road leading to Dunfermline from the west passed through Pittencrieff. A relic of this ancient highway is the famous Tower Bridge, which is shown here from below. The lower arch is the remnant of a bridge which was erected in 1611. The upper arch, which raised the level of the roadway, dates from 1788.

45. The path and Tower Bridge (or Double Bridge as it is also called) shown here from a different perspective. Aggie, who sent this card to an Edinburgh address in August 1905, had been 'here listening to the band yesterday afternoon'.

46. An aerial view of Dunfermline circa 1930, showing Pittencrieff House and the Glen. While the Glen Bridge (completed in 1932) does not appear, the Louise Carnegie Gates of 1929 are visible. Henry Reid & Son's Abbey Gardens Works in St. Margaret Street are still there. Until it shut its doors in 1928, this firm produced linen 'woven under the very walls of the Royal Palace of Dunfermline' (see illustrations 69 and 70). The factory was not demolished till some years later. This particular postcard was one of the 'Herbert' Series, published by a well-known local bookseller and stationer: Herbert T. Macpherson.

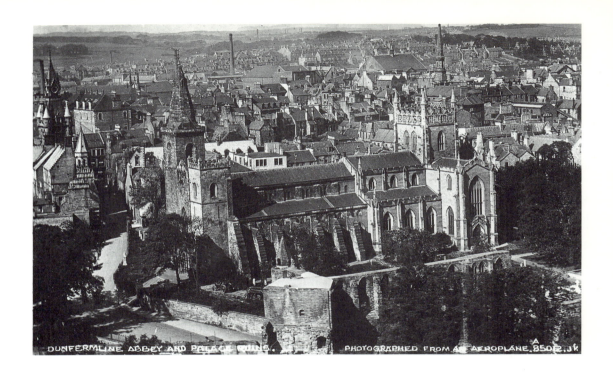

47. Another 'Herbert' Series aerial postcard, pinpointing the abbey and palace ruins. An early tractor or traction-engine is visible within the kirkyard, adjacent to the south-west tower. Close beside it is a waggon loaded with tree-trunks. Other trees that have been cut down are lying on the grass nearby. As with the previous aerial view, factory chimneys and weaving sheds were prominent features in the townscape of that period.

48. This card depicts the abbey and, in the foreground, a group of old houses which stood on the west side of St. Catherine's Wynd. In 1907 these buildings were knocked down, and a parapet wall, with wrought-iron railings and gate, was erected to enhance the appearance of the Glen. Although carried out on the advice of Sir Robert Lorimer, a distinguished Scottish architect, the demolition by the Carnegie Dunfermline Trustees of this picturesque group of old dwellings raised a lot of ire. Some critics accused the Trust of architectural vandalism. This is yet another of the 'Herbert' Series of postcards. It is worth noting that Herbert T. Macpherson was issuing, in this instance, an outdated postcard. Macpherson did not set up shop in Dunfermline till 1915 – eight years after the buildings shown in the postcard had been demolished.

FRATERS HALL, DUNFERMLINE.

49. Anyone seeking to emulate these three auld bodies would find it rather difficult nowadays, since the floor-level of the frater, as the monks' dining-hall was termed, was lowered in the early 1920s. The tree-trunks, referred to in the caption to postcard No. 47, were in all probability cut down at the same time as the vegetation which then, as this view of the frater shows, grew so luxuriantly.

50. Although now pedestrianised, the route through the Pends was until recent years one of the main thoroughfares into the town. Although a busy road by Edwardian standards, it would appear that the carter has halted for a while for the convenience of the photographer looking down from the kirkyard.

51. Unlike the working carter shown in the previous illustration, the sender of this card (postmark date 1906) described himself as 'still one of the unemployed'. Since St. Margaret's Cave, which is illustrated here, was once a place for prayer and pilgrimage, one wonders if the sender had himself visited the cave in quest of celestial guidance. Now situated beneath a car-park, this is the cave, where, according to tradition, Queen Margaret sought seclusion for private prayer. The cave, with an added historical display, will be open to the public in 1993 – the 900th anniversary of her death.

52. Queen Margaret, who was canonised in 1249, is depicted here surmounting the burgh coat of arms. This ornate and rather free representation of the Dunfermline crest was produced by an English firm, Ja-Ja, which specialised in heraldic postcards. In Edwardian days heraldic cards of this type were exceedingly popular.

53. Coming back now to the town centre via the Kirkgate, we observe that this is a very old photograph, since it shows the auld toon-hoose which was demolished about 1876 to make way for the present-day more ornate town-house. We already noted that this street was an important artery of traffic, which helps to explain the presence of the two inns shown in the left foreground. Both inns have been greatly altered. While the historic Old Inn has retained its name, its neighbour to the south, the Abbey Tavern, has been given a new name.

54. In Queen Anne Street, right in the heart of the town, the pawnbroker's premises provided a valued facility. In 1913 James Mullan advertised: 'Money to Lend... Prompt Advances made on Jewellery, Pianos, Organs, Guns, Sewing Machines, and all Articles of Value.' In addition to his shop in Queen Anne Street and another in Chapel Street, James Mullan owned pawnshops in Cowdenbeath and Inverkeithing. The watches, keeper-rings and other items, displayed in this circa 1925 photograph, would have been someone's treasures – pawned in times of hardship. We wonder if there is a story behind the boxing-gloves hanging beneath the lamp on the left. This building, which was on the south side of Queen Anne Street, was demolished to make way for the Kingsgate shopping centre.

55. The street shown here was another former stage-coach route – this time a northern exit from the town. When this photograph was taken, this section of the thoroughfare was called Bath Street – the name deriving from the ornately-fronted edifice on the right. Andrew Carnegie gifted this building, the town's first baths, to the people of Dunfermline in 1877. In 1913, the year after Aggie posted this card to Wallyford, the name was changed. Bath Street became part of the already existing Pilmuir Street.

56. After he retired from active business, Andrew Carnegie devoted himself to acts of philanthropy. Dunfermline was a major beneficiary, its gifts including a new, larger, and more imposing baths – gifted in 1902 and opened for use in 1905. A guide-book of the time informs us that 'for the small sum of 2d, visitors are admitted to view the palatial establishment, considered the finest in the kingdom'.

57. To make way for the new baths, the cottages on the right-hand of the picture were demolished during or just prior to 1902. Andrew Reid & Co.'s Pilmuir Works on the opposite side of the road was one of the town's major linen mills. In 1926 it was acquired by Hay and Robertson. Is the tradesman on the scaffolding, at the extreme left-hand side, working on the building improvements which, we know, were carried out in 1901?

58. Now we see the interior of the new Carnegie Baths. In this 1930s photograph, we observe that the changing cubicles were then sited at the side of the pool. The gable windows stand open – presumably to remove the steam rising from the shower-rooms below.

59. The Dunfermline High School boys shown above had won the Lauder Challenge Trophy for life-saving and swimming. The trophy had been presented that year, 1910, for competition by Miss Elizabeth S. Lauder. That same year, Kathleen Keir, on the right, won the Lauder Cup, also a gold medal, for swimming and life-saving. The runner-up, Jean Hamilton, was awarded a silver medal. Notice the contrast in dress between the two photographs. Whereas the boys appear in their swimsuits, the girls have to wear gym-slips over their costumes.

60. The Baths building also included a billiard room with three tables and Turkish baths. Note the pseudo-Turkish influence in the interior design of the dressing-room. Hot Bovril, as the wall placards indicate, was sold in these premises – presumably to reinvigorate any bathers who felt weak after a session in the sweatbox.

61. Another feature that attracted attention was this well-equipped gymnasium. Notice the spectators' gallery and, on a more ominous note, the stretcher propped against the wall on the left.

62. Opened in 1912 by Louise Carnegie, the Womens' Institute in Pilmuir Street incorporated a social parlour and reading-room. The Institute was open to all women and girls of Dunfermline for 'a nominal yearly subscription'. This card, conveying the message that the sender was going to Lassodie on the following day, was posted in the evening (the postmark time is 8.15 p.m.). The sender took it for granted, however, that the card would be delivered in time.

63. The Lauder Technical School (later College) was gifted to the town by Andrew Carnegie. It was named, at Andrew's request, to commemorate his uncle George Lauder, who, he said, 'was really the spirit which produced the school'. Part of the former Dunfermline High School building, opened in 1886, appears on the left. A rather unexciting car park nowadays covers the rockery-garden shown in the foreground. Presently unoccupied and no longer used for educational purposes, these two buildings will be given, if current plans are implemented, a new lease of life.

64. Situated on the south side of Nethertown Broad Street, the three-storey building shown here was replaced by the Netherton Institute which, although partially completed in 1914, was not finished until the war ended in 1918. This tenement, known as Botany House, had been built around 1760, partly from stones from the auld Palace. The scene of a child-murder in 1794, the tenement was subsequently haunted by 'the wean-ghaist'. The name, Botany House, derives from the same period when one of the lodgers, an old soldier, threatened, when drunk, 'death and vengeance' to his neighbours, even though he might risk transportation to Botany Bay.

65. A close-up view of the Botany House advertisement posters. Whyte & Co. of Bonnar Street were offering reduced-price pianos and organs in a stock-taking sale. The public were also being encouraged to purchase the 'Dunfermline Express'. Founded in 1900, the 'Express' was incorporated in the 'West Fife Echo' in 1926. Prospective emigrants would no doubt have been interested in the numerous steam-ship line posters. The German Norddeutscher Lloyd Line for one was offering cheap fares to Australia – a rather ironic touch for a building which was popularly known as Botany House. The lower photograph shows the same group of buildings, this time from the rear. By the late 19th century Botany House was described as still possessing 'the decayed appearance of a past respectability but is now descended into the sere and yellow leaf of a fourth-rate dwelling'. Part of the roof of the Dunfermline and West Fife Hospital can be seen in the background.

66. The Dunfermline Cottage Hospital, which was opened in 1894, was, after being considerably extended, transformed into the Dunfermline and West Fife Hospital in 1905. As was usual in those days, it was a voluntary hospital paid for by public subscription. With the completion of a new District Hospital, the existing complex is due to close in 1993.

67. Opened in 1883 by Lord Rosebery, a Lothian landowner and future Prime Minister, the Gothic-style Public Library was the first of the many Carnegie Free Libraries. The gas lamp at the corner, which is long gone, would have illuminated the inscription above the door which very appropriately reads: 'Let there be light.'

68. Innovatory in a number of ways, the Carnegie Dunfermline Trust encouraged children to learn gardening. Part of the ground chosen for this purpose is shown in this early 20th century photograph. The particular area shown lies to the south of Rose Crescent. As there was no question of the children losing school-time for this, the bairns tended their allotments after school hours, with the Pittencrieff Park gardeners supervising their efforts. Prizes were given for the best-kept plots.

69. Interior of Henry Reid and Sons' Abbey Gardens Linen factory in St. Margaret Street. This factory closed in 1928. In the foreground is Andrew Inches, who was employed as a loom tenter. Although three men are shown in this photograph, the great majority of the employees were actually women. The site was later used as a bus station. On the right is Andrew Inches in off-duty pose. Dressed in his 'Sunday suit', he stands with his wife, Margaret, and daughter Jean, ready for the photographer. Margaret Inches reached the ripe old age of 97. After the Abbey Works closed down, Andrew, though a skilled worker, remained unemployed for eight years. Many other workers in the by then collapsing linen industry shared a similar fate.

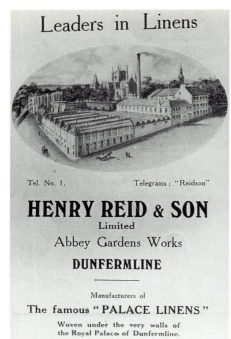 

70. Andrew Inches was still in their employment when Henry Reid and Sons placed this advertisement in a mid-1920s guide-book. Novelty postcards were another popular advertising device – like this linen heraldic card inscribed 'Frae the Linen City.'

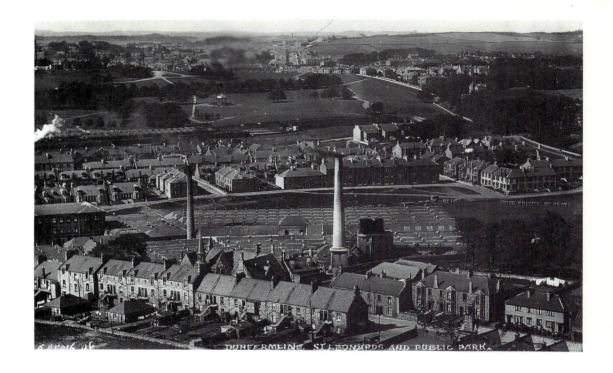

71. This 1920s aerial photograph reveals how large these linen works could be. The two tall smokestacks of Erskine Beveridge's Linen Works dominate the foreground scene. Only the office and warehouse building still survives, that block having been converted into flats. Bisected by a new dual carriage-way, the Public Park at the top of the picture has likewise undergone considerable alteration.

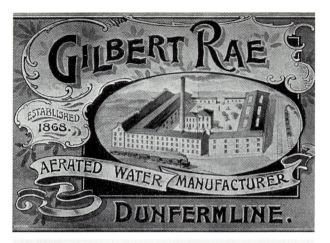

## GILBERT RAE,

IF you have not given my Waters a trial, please do so; they are certain to give you satisfaction.

All Orders entrusted to the Agents shall be promptly executed.

The Works cover four acres of Floorage, are worked by a powerful Steam-Engine, and lighted throughout by Electricity.

Aerated Water Manufacturer, DUNFERMLINE.

72. While there is a measure of artistic licence in this sketch, it does convey the message – namely that Gilbert Rae's lemonade factory is an important and modern manufacturing establishment. As this advertisement leaflet shows, the factory chimney and the steam-train for transporting the finished product were potent symbols of the age of steam. And, as the text makes plain, the works were even 'lighted throughout by Electricity'.

73. For those who despised aerated waters, Brown's Brewery, in what later became known as the Regal Close, supplied a more potent form of liquid refreshment. In this late-Victorian photograph we see the bowler-hatted proprietor seated in the centre, surrounded by his all-male staff. The company's sign proudly displayed is a fine example of the signwriter's art. The brewery survived until at least the end of the 19th century. In later years, there was a bakery in this area, Craig's, whose premises were incorporated in the bookshop and stationery business of Herbert T. Macpherson, whose publications included the 'Herbert' Series of postcards.

74. In the early 1920s Townhill Road was, as now, an important access road. It was crossed by the railway line which led from Dunfermline to Stirling and, incidentally, also served Gilbert Rae's Aerated Water factory. The railway bridge, which is just beyond the tram-car, has now gone – likewise the buildings and the advertising hoardings on the left.

75. The tram-car shown in the left-hand picture would have been serviced at the tram-depot, St. Leonard's Street, where this group of workers was employed. The tram on the right, car 43, was one of a number delivered in April 1918 for use on the Dunfermline to Rosyth route. Whilst this car displays a rather prosaic advert for High Street ironmongers James Bonnar & Sons, the other tram carries a rather more enticing advertisement. It reads: *If you are pleasure bound / the La Scala / is the place to find it.* Unfortunately, the La Scala Picture House on Guildhall Street was destroyed by fire on Sunday, 13th April 1924. Hazarding a guess at occupations, the hatless man standing in the back row is one of the office staff, as are at least two of the girls. The girl on the left, judging by her dress, may well be a cleaner. Is the smartly dressed young lad in knickerbockers an office boy? The paint-bespattered jackets of the two men on his left leave little doubt as to their particular trade.

76. The coming of the automobile and the motor-bus heralded the doom of the tram-car as far as Dunfermline was concerned. We have here a 1920s view of John Jackson's Coach Works in Pittencrieff Street. Some decades later, one of the co-authors served his apprenticeship as a coach-builder there, although the canvas-topped bus, which Jackson built, was well before his time.

77. Motor-buses also put horse-drawn passenger vehicles off the roads. The coach with the party of sightseers, photographed near the Palace, was owned by the Kirkcaldy-based Fife Posting Company. Mr. Finlayson, the driver, resided in Aberdour.

78. The increase in the number of motor vehicles necessitated improvements to the road network. The Glen Bridge, for example, was opened in 1932. Observe on the skyline, in the top illustration, the numerous works chimneys. In the lower view, looking west to Pittencrieff Street, we see no fewer than three early 1930s buses.

79. On match days the buses were kept busy, ferrying football supporters to East End Park. In this earlier, Edwardian-period photograph we see Dunfermline Athletic, the local favourites, in typical manly pose. At that time the Pars played in the Northern League. Their corrugated iron changing hut is a far cry from today's grandstand, but it was no doubt all that the Club could afford. That same year, the Club Treasurer lamented, their finances were in a parlous state, owing to the high cost of railway fares. The Club ended that season with a balance of 16/7 d (in today's coinage about 83 pence). At least, unlike many clubs today, Dunfermline was not in the red. Following their triumph in the Qualifying Cup in 1911, the Club was, in the following year, admitted to the Scottish League, joining a Second Division that had been extended from 12 to 14 clubs. There are no women to be seen, football being then regarded as a masculine preserve.

80. The boundary fence of East End Park comes into this early 1920s view of Halbeath Road looking to the west. When the road was widened around 1924, a brick wall replaced this ramshackle barrier. It is interesting to note that there is no pavement on the football-ground side, just a dirt track. The tramway lines, of course, had to be firmly bedded-in with granite setts.

81. Golf was another popular form of recreation. The Venturefair course of the Canmore Club, founded in 1898, was more accessible than the older Dunfermline Golf Club's course, which was then located at North Queensferry. We note that the golfers carry very few clubs and that they tee up the ball using sand from the sandbox.

82. It was the prosperous middle-classes who financed the construction of golf-courses and clubhouses. They too pioneered in using the motor-car as a means of private transport, although, as here, they usually employed a chauffeur to drive and maintain their cars. The gentleman shown here was a local doctor – Dr. Peter Sturrock.

83. H. Williamson, the chauffeur shown in the previous photograph, appears again in this picnic scene. It is the year 1915, and the picnic, rather unusually, is in his honour. He is being entertained by his employer and family because he is leaving for war service.

84. Vonda Sturrock, the girl shown in the picnic group, appears in this obviously earlier photograph, too. This unusual interior view shows her using her father's microscope. It is interesting to note that her elbow rests on the 'Manual of General Pathology'.

85. These girls, contemporaries of Vonda Sturrock, were pupils at the old Commercial School, but shown in this 1912 photograph wearing their summer frocks and dancing in Pittencrieff Park. The school gym teacher, a Miss Armour, arranged a dancing class on a voluntary basis. The girl on the left, with upraised arm, is Jean Ritchie, who in 1992 celebrated her 90th birthday in Dunfermline.

86. The year is 1895, the place is Kincardine on Forth; and here is P.C. John Brown standing in the High Street beside the 17th century market cross which, incidentally, is surmounted by the Keith coat of arms. There is not much happening on this particular morning, although the photographer's activities are obviously a matter of interest.

87. Like many other policemen in those days, P.C. Brown came from farming stock. His obvious interest in horticultural matters was maintained while serving with Fife Constabulary. Judging by their success at the Tulliallan 1894 Flower Show, he and his wife, Betsy, were clearly skilful gardeners. John Brown, it is worth remarking, was the first of three generations of police officers who served with Fife Constabulary, one rising to the rank of Chief Constable.

88. The gentleman shown here is a local clergyman – photographed in what nowadays would be called leisure wear. He was D.P. Thomson, who was minister at Gillespie Church in Dunfermline from 1928 to 1934. As one of the leading evangelists of the day, the Reverend D.P. Thomson established a number of centres for use as retreats and for accommodating conferences. A simple cottage at Glassiebarns by Craigluscar was procured and was used for this purpose by the Gillespie Church congregation. Above we see a very large group from the Dunfermline congregation outside the Glassiebarns retreat. 'D.P.' himself is in the centre. The Glassiebarns but-and-ben (now a ruin incidentally) was very small, so in 1932 a new centre was opened at Lassodie west of Kelty.

*United Free Church, Lassodie.*

89. When the Lassodie population declined, the former United Free Church and manse were left empty. D.P. Thomson took over the kirk and used it for some years as a conference-centre and retreat, renaming it St. Ninians. Incidentally, the name St. Ninians was given to other centres established in later years by this forceful evangelist. When in the late 1930s Hitler's forces went on the march, refugees from Nazi-occupied Europe were housed in the church. The kirk was demolished after the war. In its palmy days, prior to the First World War, Lassodie was a thriving mining community. After its four pits closed, it became virtually a ghost village. When Lassodie Colliery closed in 1931, the owners, Messrs. Thomas Spowart & Co. Ltd., gave the miners and their families 14 days to vacate their company houses. The New Rows, like the rest of the miners' rows, were eventually demolished.

*NEW ROWS, LASSODIE.*

90. The pupils or, in contemporary parlance, the 'scholars' of Lassodie School photographed in 1909 during the heyday of the village. Although the boys have doffed their caps, the girls are all wearing hats or bonnets. The local milliners evidently did quite good trade. If we can judge by the surface indications of a formally-posed photograph, this was not a poverty-stricken community. One cannot say, however, that they look very happy! Perhaps, though, some of the boys went on to star for the successful Lassodie Juveniles football team – one of this lively community's many societies and clubs. These included a Horticultural Society, a Homing Pigeon Society, Brass band, Ambulance Class, Golf Club and Burns Literary Club. Since these appear to be essentially in the male domain, perhaps the girls and women were kept too busy with domestic chores.

91. Some of the children's parents would have served in the Lassodie Mines Rescue Team. Wearing a primitive form of breathing apparatus, the miners are fully kitted out and are ready for the off. The car was supplied by one of the pit owners. Since in the early 1900s none of the miners would have known how to drive, the services of his chauffeur were also required.

KELTY MOTOR TRANSPORT Co.    13

## FOOTBALL FIXTURES.

| DATE. | OPPONENTS. | | FOR | AG. | PTS. |
|---|---|---|---|---|---|

### Dunfermline.

**1927.**
Aug. 13—Motherwell ... away
„   20—Airdrie ... home
„   27—Partick Thistle away
Sept. 3—St. Mirren ... home
„   10—Hearts ... away
„   17—Celtic ... home
„   24—Bo'ness ... away
Oct. 1—St. Johnstone ... home
„   8—Aberdeen ... away
„   15—Cowdenbeath ... home
„   22—Hamilton ... away
„   29—Dundee ... home
Nov. 5—Rangers ... home
„   12—Clyde ... away
„   19—Raith Rovers ... home
„   26—Queen's Park ... home
Dec. 3—Falkirk ... away
„   10—Kilmarnock ... away
„   17—Hibernians ... home
„   24—Motherwell ... home
„   31—St. Mirren ... away
**1928.**
Jan. 2—Cowdenbeath ... away
„   3—Hearts ... home
„   7—Partick Thistle home
„   14—Celtic ... away
„   28—Aberdeen ... home

92. Some of the regulars at the Lassodie Tavern no doubt supported Dunfermline Athletic. All the clubs mentioned in this football fixture list are still in existence, although Bo'ness is now a Junior League team having been expelled from senior football in 1932, being unable to meet match guarantees. For the record, in season 1927-28, Bo'ness and Dunfermline finished in second-last and last position respectively.

93. The fixture list shown opposite was published by the Kelty Motor Transport Company, whose buses operated on the Lassodie to Dunfermline run. This evocative 1920s photograph shows their first bus. One of the co-owners, William Mclean, stands beside his Maudslay bus. He wears boots and leather leggings which were standard wear for drivers of both horse-drawn and motor-engined vehicles. Notice the large starting-handle. The driver would have had to acquire the knack of 'swinging' the handle. Otherwise, if he was not careful, he ran the risk of breaking his thumb. The solid rubber tyres meant that passenger comfort must have been minimal. Rather intriguingly, the bus has two types of light. While the headlamps would have been battery-operated, the side lights seem to be the acetylene type.

94. Culross on the Forth was another place linked to Dunfermline by means of a regular bus service. Many of the people shown in this circa 1900 illustration are, however, excursionists. Their horse-drawn char-à-bancs have stopped on the Sandhaven outside the 17th century Townhouse. Later visitors had an alternative means of transport, when the Dunfermline to Kincardine railway line opened in July 1906. As well as Culross, Cairneyhill and Torryburn were served by this line.

95. The old-world town of Culross has long been a tourist destination, with the 'Palace', shown here, being one of the prime attractions. Now in the care of the National Trust for Scotland, the Palace was originally the home of Sir George Bruce. He developed, around 1700, the remarkable Moat Pit, whose coal workings stretched beneath the waters of the Firth of Forth.

96./97. Going eastward from Culross, we arrive at Rosyth. In 1903 the government of the day selected Rosyth as the site of a new deep-water naval base. The new base was built close to Rosyth Castle which, when these photographs were taken, was a popular bathing and picnic spot. Now it is wholly within the naval base.

Rosyth Castle, Dunfermline.

These pictures show the strongly-built tower, which dates back to the 15th century, and the surviving fragments of the 16th/17th century courtyard. Damaged by Cromwell's soldiers in 1651, it was in decay by the beginning of the 18th century. It is possible to visit the castle, but special permission is required.

Rosyth Naval Base
Is admitted to be a most complete Naval Dockyard in every respect. It lies within easy reach of extensive coal fields and has exceptional railway facilities. About sixteen miles within the estuary of the Forth it is well protected by modern fortifications.

98. This postcard shows an artist's impression of the projected base. It was the naval threat posed by an increasingly powerful German fleet, that brought the British Admiralty to the Firth of Forth. The Firth provided sheltered waters and, at the same time, was conveniently situated for North Sea patrols. Work commenced in 1909, the main contractors being Messrs. Easton, Gibb & Son Ltd. It was not, however, until 1916, two years after the war started, that the first warship – H.M.S. 'Zealandia' – was docked and repaired at Rosyth.

99. Newspaper vendors are doing good trade in this all-male scene at the dockyard gates. No cars are to be seen in this circa 1920 view, but there are plenty of bikes. One wonders how many workers ignored the prominently displayed No Smoking Order.

100. The Rosyth dry docks were constructed at great expense to house and repair the largest vessels in the British fleet. Completed in 1914, the 27,000 ton H.M.S. 'Tiger' – seen here in No. 2 Dock – was the largest of the British battle-cruisers. This stern view shows two of her eight powerful 13.5 inch guns. H.M.S. 'Tiger' fought in the battles of the Dogger Bank in 1915 and Jutland in the following year. In the running sea-fight of the Dogger Bank, the 'Tiger' was hit six times by German shells, but she in turn inflicted very little damage on the enemy, her shooting being afterwards described as abysmal.

H.M.S. "Lion". H.M.S. "Princess Royal". H.M.S. "Temaraire". with Cranes in Background, East End No 3 Dock. Rosyth.

101. Another two vessels from Admiral Beatty's First Battle-cruiser Squadron appear in this view – the 'Lion', Beatty's flagship, and the 'Princess Royal'. The 'Queen Mary', from the same class of ship, was one of three British battle-cruisers destroyed at Jutland, which was by far the greatest of the First World War sea-battles.

102. Flying the flag of the dashing Admiral Beatty (shown in inset), H.M.S. 'Lion' was the pride of the fleet. Although very fast and, thanks to her eight 13.5 inch guns, packing a massive punch, her deck-armour, as with the other British battle-cruisers, was inadequate, resulting in the heavy loss of ships and men at Jutland. The 'Lion' herself was badly damaged and 99 of her crew were killed. The grandfather of co-author George Robertson was one of the crew who survived this epic battle. He was a stoker, serving on the 'Lion' for most of the war and helping to fuel her 70,000 horse-power engines.

POWER STATION WITH CLOCK AND BATTERY SHEDS, ROSYTH DOCKYARD.

103. A huge industrial site like Rosyth required its own power station. The chimney with its large clock was a notable landmark.

104./105. Workmen's Bungalow City was the rather grandiose name for the village erected to house incoming workers and their families. Tintown was the more familiar name given to the new village. The name was derived from the corrugated iron cladding used in the construction of the village. Interestingly, both these postcards present two versions of the same view. The original, and probably untouched, postcard is the one above, which shows Tintown West, at its extreme south-west corner looking north-east. The postcard on the right has

been 'improved' by being tinted and touched up, with flowers added to the gardens. The prominent post in the centre may look like a gallows, but is in fact a lamp standard. This particular card was sent in May 1915 to a naval stoker on board H.M.S. 'Dreadnought', which was the first of the modern battleships that transformed naval warfare in the early years of the 20th century. Since the ship's whereabouts were a military secret, the card was addressed c/o the GPO, London.

106. Overall view of Tintown West – the photograph was taken in Hilton Road looking north-east. The village was built prior to the First World War by the contractors Easton Gibb & Son Ltd.

107. A close-up view of Tintown – date probably around 1915. Note the large, untidy and litter-bestrewn hedgerow. The pinafores of the girls in the front are rather grubby, but the children look healthy enough.

108. The Tintown children, judging from the previous photograph, were well enough shod. Their boots and shoes were no doubt repaired at this local shoe-repair establishment. Wall posters advertise British Boot Polish.

109. The spiritual needs of the new community were catered for no less than the material. With many key workers coming to Rosyth from England, this Wesleyan Methodist Church was one of the early buildings in the new village. Built in 1916, this timber-construction building closed in 1926, by which time the dockyard was operated on a care-and-maintenance basis only. The Reverend Charlesworth was the first clergyman and he served until 1920. He was succeeded by the Reverend Porri.

110. Here is another, even larger group of Rosyth children, some in Scout uniform, lined up on the Recreation Ground at Bungalow City West. The man on the extreme right, next to the Scoutmaster, is William J. Seaman. A civil engineer employed by Alexander Gibb, Seaman, it is believed, was responsible for the building of the houses shown here. The large building in the background was a mission-hall, which doubled as a school. The dockyard power station chimney (picture No. 103) is visible in the background.

111. The growth in population during the 1914-1918 war meant that new schools had to be built. Some of the Rosyth bairns attended the Inverkeithing 'Tinschool', another temporary structure. It was located near Inverkeithing Railway Station at the Chapel Place junction.

112. This is King's Road School. The name given to the school in the caption to the postcard (King George Schools) is presumably a printer's error. King's Road School was opened in April 1918, the first headmaster being Major R.W. Wallace. In the foreground can be seen the track of the tram route between Dunfermline and Rosyth Dockyard. The trams commenced running in May, 1918.

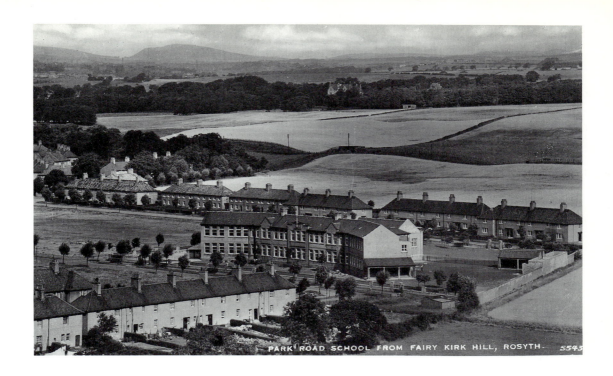

113. Park Road was, and still is, a Primary school. The permanent houses built in Rosyth Garden Suburb were much superior to the Tintown dwellings. Since this photograph was taken, more houses have been built. The farmland shown here has been bisected by the motorway spur to Dunfermline. Pitreavie Castle, now a military establishment, is in the background.

114. Opened during the First World War, the Rosyth Brick & Tile Company provided the raw materials for the new, permanent schools and houses of Rosyth Garden City. With many local men in the services, the company was allocated a number of German prisoners of war – five of whom are visible in the foreground. This particular enterprise continued till the early 1930s. As the photograph indicates, the machine-house with its lofty lum and the drying-shed on the right were sizeable buildings. The clay-pit is now a reservoir.

115. Rosyth Halt Railway Station is located on the Dunfermline to Inverkeithing line. It was opened in 1917 by the North British Railway Company. The station hasn't changed much, except for the removal of the signal box in the foreground.

116./117. Two mid-1920s postcards. The first of Queensferry Road is looking south; the second of Admiralty Road is looking to the east. There were few traffic problems in those days. The vehicle appearing in the fore-

ground of both photographs is the same car. Most likely it was the photographer's own vehicle. Macari's ice-cream cart was no doubt popular with the children.

118. Surprise, surprise! Here is the same car again – registration number CP 9295 – on Woodside Avenue near its junction with Leslie Road. The wooded area to the right was known locally as Wilderness Wood – a perfect natural playground for local children.

119. We see here Woodside Street, Rosyth, looking north. The delivery horse and cart belonged to Binning, butcher and poulterer, Inverkeithing.

120. Binning, we deduce from this photograph, had competitors – in this case John Scott from Dunfermline. The smartly turned-out vanman is J. Anderson. This early 1920s photograph was taken on Park Road at its junction with Queensferry Road.

121. This is Queensferry Road in the 1920s looking south-west, with on the left the proposed route of a tram-line which was never completed. In the background we see a coal delivery cart. The other horse-drawn vehicle is a van – possibly a bakery van – owned by Dick's Cooperative Institutions.

122. We are still in Queensferry Road. This seems to be a well-stocked shop with a variety of provisions for sale. As it was situated opposite the Palace Picture House, sweeties and cigarettes would have sold very well.

123. The potted palms add an exotic touch to the lounge of the Rosyth Institute, which opened in 1926. Most of the readers, in this all-male gathering, are wearing bunnets.

124. To redress the balance, and ending on a lighter note, we show a ladies' dance band. We see them in the Palais de Danse, a popular place of entertainment in Rosyth during the 1920s. All the entertainers belong to the same local family – three daughters with their parents. While Mrs. Williams plays the piano, her husband, who is in charge of the group, stands looking on from the rear. The hall was situated in Park Road, where the long-established Will's Garage is now located. It is just visible behind the horse's head in picture No. 120.